Your Body for Life

Your Physical Body

From birth to old age

Anne Rooney

Heinemann
LIBRARY

Chicago, Illinois

Edited by Andrew Farrow, Adam Miller, and Adrian Vigliano

Designed by Cynthia Della-Rovere

Original illustrations © Capstone Global Library Ltd.

Illustrated by HL Studios Ltd.

Picture research by Mica Brancic

Production by Victoria Fitzgerald

Originated by Capstone Global Library Ltd.

Printed and bound in China by Leo Paper Products Ltd.

16 15 14 13 12

10 9 8 7 6 5 4 3 2 1

Library of Congress Cataloging-in-Publication Data

Rooney, Anne.

 Your physical body : from birth to old age / Anne Rooney.

  p. cm.—(Your body for life)

Includes bibliographical references and index.

 ISBN 978-1-4329-7087-1 (hb)—ISBN 978-1-4329-7094-9 (pb)
1. Human growth. 2. Life cycle, Human. I. Title.

 QP84.R66 2013

 612—dc23   2012014553

Acknowledgments

The author and publishers are grateful to the following for
permission to reproduce copyright material: Alamy pp. 7 (©
Chad Ehlers), 11 (© Sally and Richard Greenhill), 19 (© Mike
Abrahams), 24 (© Scott Camazine), 28 (© Classic Image), 31
(© Custom Medical Stock Photo), 39 (© Corbis Flirt/Randy
Faris), 44 (© Megapress), 47 (© Alex Ekins), 49 (© Zefa RF/
Sebastian Pfuetze), 52 (© Malo-Image); Corbis pp. 22 (Design
Pics/© Rowan Gillson), 33 (National Geographic Society/©
Steve Winter), 34 (© PCN), 54 (© Benelux); Getty Images p. 9
(Hulton Archive); Science Photo Library p. 17 left (A J Photo);
Shutterstock pp. 4 (© Thomas M Perkins), 15 (© Reynardt), 36
(© Piotr Marcinski), 40 (© Tish1), 51 (© Galushko Sergey), 17
right (© Konmesa).

Cover photograph of X-ray background reproduced with
permission of iStockphoto (© NI QIN).

Cover photograph of X-rays reproduced with permission of
Shutterstock (© jannoon028).

We would like to thank David Wright for his invaluable help in
the preparation of this book.

Every effort has been made to contact copyright holders of
any material reproduced in this book. Any omissions will
be rectified in subsequent printings if notice is given to the
publisher.

Disclaimer

Contents

Some words are printed in **bold**, like this. You can find out what they mean by looking in the glossary on page 60.

From Cradle to Grave

If you compare yourself to your grandparents, you will see that you look very different. This is because our bodies undergo huge changes as we go through life.

Always changing

Your body works hard at all ages to carry out seven basic life processes common to all living things: movement, sensitivity, **excretion**, **nutrition**, **respiration**, growth, and **reproduction**. Its work changes with time, though.

From baby to adult

A tiny baby's body concentrates on gaining nourishment and growing. An adult's body is at its physical peak and should be healthy and active. With advancing age, further changes take place and the body works less well.

Fuel for the body

To grow and move, the body needs **nutrients** from food and oxygen from the air. Your body is mostly made up from four basic substances called elements: oxygen (65 percent), carbon (18 percent), hydrogen (10 percent), and nitrogen (3 percent). Calcium (1.5 percent) and phosphorous (1 percent) are also vital. These building blocks make up 99 percent of the body.

The elements are arranged into lots of different chemical combinations making compounds such as water, **fats**, **proteins**, and other substances. Food is made of compounds which the body breaks down, reusing the components to build chemicals the body needs.

Inside and outside

Some of the changes in the body are easy to see. Over time, babies grow larger and the proportions of the body change—the head becomes comparatively smaller and the limbs are longer. Other changes began at **puberty**: people grow body hair, and their reproductive systems start to work. Elderly people might be stooped, with wrinkled skin and gray hair—clear changes from when they were younger. There are also changes inside the body, which we cannot see. Older people often have brittle bones, which break easily. You cannot see brittle bones, but the effects are painful.

What are you made of?

There are four main types of **tissue** that make up your body: muscle, nerve, connective, and epithelial tissue. Muscles support the body and enable it to move. Nerves carry information to, from, and within the brain. Connective tissue gives structure and support to the body or connects parts together, and it includes bone and blood. Epithelial tissue provides linings and surfaces, such as the skin and the lining of the intestines.

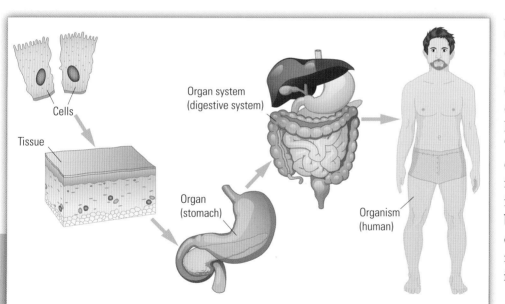

Cells

Tissue

Organ system
(digestive system)

Organ
(stomach)

Organism
(human)

All these tissues are made from **cells**. There are very many different types of cell in the human body. The structure of each type is suited to its function. A blood cell is very different from a muscle cell, for instance.

Cells, tissues, organs, bodies

The body contains organs and structures made of tissue of different types. All these tissues are made from cells. Each type has a structure suited to its own function.

AMAZING BUT TRUE!

Crawling with life

There are about 10 trillion (10,000,000,000,000) human cells in an adult's body—and 10 times as many extra tiny living things in and on it! Most of these tiny living things cause no harm, and many actually help the body. **Bacteria** in the stomach and intestines help break down our food, for example.

A Brand New Body

The human body grows and develops for 38 weeks before being born. The period before birth is actually when the body grows most quickly.

Starting from scratch

A new baby begins when a **sperm** cell from the father and an egg cell from the mother come together, and the sperm **fertilizes** the egg. The fertilized egg divides into two, and then those two cells divide again, making four cells, and so on. Every new cell contains an exact copy of the **genetic** information in the fertilized egg.

To start with, all the cells are the same—they are called **stem cells**. They can become any part of the growing baby. Around a week after fertilization, when the group of cells is about the size of the dot over this letter "i," the cells start to differentiate. This means they start forming different types of tissue and grow into the organs and structures of the body. At this stage, the baby is called an **embryo**. After eight weeks, when it is recognizably human, it is called a **fetus**. You can see in detail how the embryo and fetus grow on pages 58 and 59.

More than one!

Sometimes the mother's body releases two eggs, and both are fertilized. Fraternal twins (twins who are not identical) then develop. Identical twins occur if a single fertilized egg splits into two separate embryos early in its development. Identical twins have the same genetic material, since they are from a single fertilized egg.

AMAZING BUT TRUE!

Eggs to spare

A female embryo at 11 weeks has around two million eggs in her body, meaning she will be ready to have her own babies later. At birth, the number will have dropped to one million eggs, and by age 17 she will have only 200,000. Only around 500 eggs will ever be released and have the chance of being fertilized.

How the unborn baby grows

While the unborn baby grows, the mother's blood provides nourishment for it. The **placenta** is an organ that grows in the mother's **uterus**, forming a connection between her body and the developing baby. Mother and baby have separate circulatory systems (the heart and blood vessels). In the placenta, oxygen and nutrients pass from the mother's blood to the baby's blood. Waste passes from the baby's blood to the mother's. The baby's blood passes through the **umbilical cord** to and from the placenta, but does not mix with the mother's blood. Substances pass through the walls of the blood vessels in the placenta.

Caring for the unborn baby

The unborn baby is affected by how the mother behaves during pregnancy. Harmful chemicals including tobacco and alcohol, and radiation such as X-rays, can damage the baby, especially in the early months of pregnancy. They can cause disability or even death.

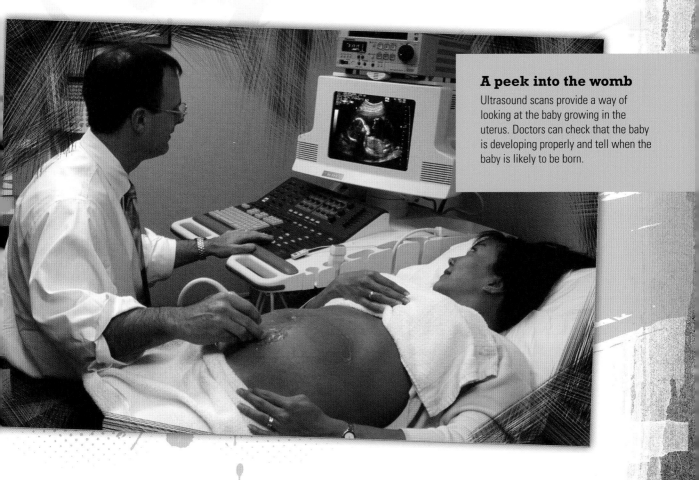

A peek into the womb

Ultrasound scans provide a way of looking at the baby growing in the uterus. Doctors can check that the baby is developing properly and tell when the baby is likely to be born.

What will the baby be like?

Each fertilized egg has 23 pairs of **chromosomes**, made up of 23 chromosomes from the sperm and 23 from the egg. Chromosomes carry all the genetic information for a person, coded on around 23,000 **genes**. The genes control growth, development, and obvious characteristics, such as hair color and skin color, and less obvious ones, such as whether people are likely to develop some kinds of cancer and the type of noise they make when they sneeze!

Not all outcomes are entirely controlled by genes. Some are influenced by factors in the environment. For instance, if a pregnant woman drinks a lot of alcohol or is exposed to other poisons, this can cause problems in the unborn baby that will affect how it grows and develops.

> *"We know there are at least 400 toxic chemicals in tobacco smoke. These can get into the pregnant mother and affect her baby."*
>
> —Dr. Jonathan Winickoff, associate professor of pediatrics at Harvard Medical School

Case study: Famine affects unborn grandchildren

It is not surprising that if there is a famine (shortage of food in an area), babies born to undernourished mothers will be harmed. But it is more surprising that grandchildren and perhaps even later generations might also be affected.

Late in World War II, in 1944–45, the German army prevented food from being delivered to Holland, leading to a famine in which 30,000 people died. People who survived the famine often had children with a low birth weight. These children had unusually high rates of **diabetes**, **obesity**, cancer, and heart disease in later life. They also gave birth to children with a low birth weight, even though they did not themselves suffer from malnutrition (lack of nutritious food) or food shortages. The genes of the malnourished parents were affected by the experience of famine, and this change passed on to future generations.

Scientists believe that the genes were affected, perhaps for three generations, to make the body hoard food in case of scarcity. When there is no scarcity, this leads to obesity and related medical conditions such as diabetes and heart disease.

When things go wrong

Around 3 in every 100 babies born alive in developed countries like the United States have major birth defects. Some defects have a lifelong impact or even lead to the death of the baby. Birth defects can be structural or functional. A structural defect occurs when part of the body is missing or wrongly formed. Most are heart defects, such as holes in the internal walls of the heart, or major **arteries** going to the wrong part of the heart. One in 150 babies born in the United States each year has a heart defect. A functional defect occurs when the baby is not able to make a chemical the body needs, usually an **enzyme** or another protein. The baby might look normal, but the body does not work properly.

Some birth defects are the result of genetic faults—either there is a defective gene that the baby inherits or something goes wrong with the baby's own genes. Others are caused by an event during pregnancy, such as the mother falling ill or being exposed to dangerous chemicals.

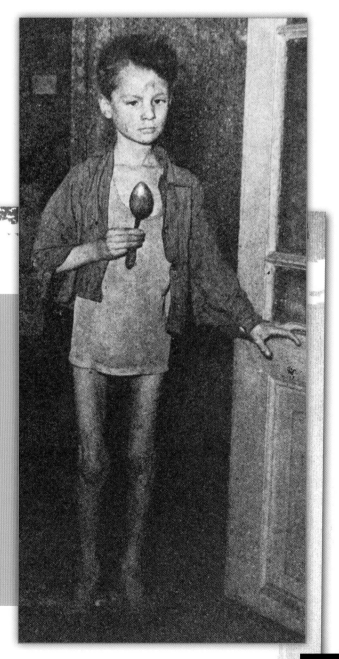

Starving in Holland

This wartime photo shows a boy who was malnourished because of food blockades in Holland in 1944-45. People who suffered during this time often went on to have children and even grandchildren affected by the changes that malnutrition caused in their bodies.

Coming into the world: Birth

After nine months, the baby is ready to be born. **Hormones** trigger the mother's muscles to contract to push the baby out through the vagina. The baby's body is adapted to help it pass through the birth canal. Many of the baby's bones and **joints** are still flexible, and the bones of the skull are not entirely fused together. During birth, the flexibility that this gives the cranium (the part of the skull that protects the brain) allows the baby's large head to squeeze through the birth canal.

The newborn is still attached to the placenta by the umbilical cord. The placenta pulls away from the wall of the uterus and is delivered after the baby. After birth, the umbilical cord is cut, and so the baby's body must take nourishment by digesting food and take oxygen from the air. Any delay in breathing endangers the baby, as the brain is starved of oxygen.

Room to move

A newborn baby has soft parts on the head where there is a gap between the plates of bone. The gaps are called fontanelles. The most noticeable is at the front of the head; it closes during the 18 months after birth.

Frontal fontanelle

Frontal fontanelle

Occipital fontanelle

Sphenoidal fontanelle

Mastoid fontanelle

Saved for later

The umbilical cord and placenta are rich in blood containing stem cells. Stem cells are unspecialized cells that can develop into different types of cell. Some hospitals save this blood for medical use or research. It is either collected in a public bank or saved for the individual baby in case it is needed in later life. Research will lead to new treatments in the future not available now. Using an individual's own stem cells for any treatment will mean that the cells are compatible with the body and will not be rejected.

Stem cells are already used to treat some blood disorders. Although using stem cells from embryos in research is a much-debated issue, using stem cells from the umbilical cord and blood is less controversial. This tissue would otherwise be thrown away, and using it does not harm the baby.

Preterm babies

A full-term baby is born after 38 weeks. Babies born before they are ready are called **preterm** babies. They sometimes have difficulty breathing because their lungs are not fully developed. A machine called a ventilator can help until the lungs develop fully.

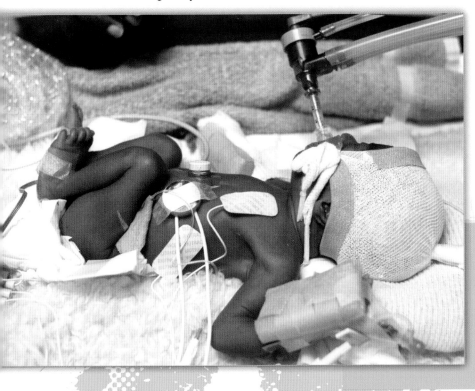

Babies born after 22 weeks of development are considered viable, which means they might be able to survive. The chances of survival at 23 weeks are around 50 percent, but some babies born this early have permanent health problems.

Preterm and tiny

In Miami, Florida, Amillia Taylor was born in 2006, after just 22 weeks and 6 days of pregnancy. She was just 9.5 inches (24 centimeters) long and weighed 10 ounces (283 grams). She is the youngest preterm baby to survive.

Getting ready for life: The seven life processes

As we have seen, the body has seven life processes: movement, sensitivity, excretion, nutrition, respiration, growth, and reproduction.

- Movement: Before birth, the fetus practices movement, exercising its muscles.
- Sensitivity: Sensitivity develops as the sense organs grow, enabling the baby to see, hear, taste, smell, and feel things immediately.
- Excretion and nutrition: Excretion and nutrition happen in the uterus, but the baby depends on the mother's body for food and to help process waste. These processes take a more familiar form after birth. The baby takes a first meal of breast milk soon after birth.
- Respiration: The baby takes its first breaths immediately after birth—the lungs are ready to work.
- Growth: The baby has been growing for 38 weeks and will continue to grow in different ways throughout life.
- Reproduction: Reproduction is the only process that is delayed. The baby's reproductive system is immature and will not be ready until puberty.

Being a Baby

In the days and weeks following birth, a baby adapts to being in the outside world and grows quickly. There is a lot for the body to do.

A day in the life of a newborn baby

The newborn baby has one main task—to grow. Growing does not mean just getting larger. It also means strengthening and developing control of muscles, fusing the bones into a rigid, supporting skeleton, and forming **neural** connections in the brain as the baby learns. The adult body uses the same methods to grow new tissue to repair damage after injury or disease.

To develop, the baby needs nourishment, oxygen from the air, stimulation, engagement with other people, affection, and a lot of sleep.

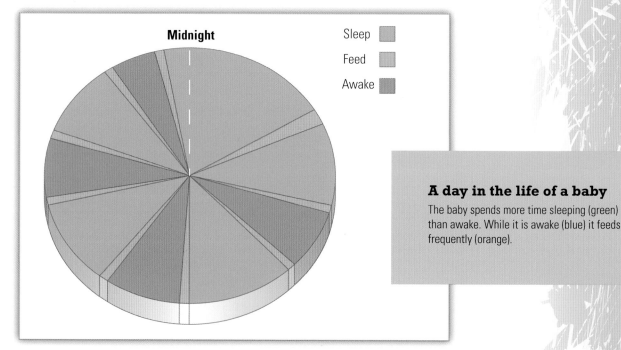

A day in the life of a baby
The baby spends more time sleeping (green) than awake. While it is awake (blue) it feeds frequently (orange).

Sleeping patterns

Newborn babies sleep around 16 hours a day, dropping to about 13 hours by the age of two. This sleep is not in a continuous block. At first, babies do not distinguish between night and day. A baby might sleep for four stretches of four hours or take eight two-hour naps. This is very exhausting for the baby's parents and can put a strain on family life.

During sleep, a baby's brain probably consolidates learning and grows neural connections. The body grows and heals itself during sleep, too.

Milk is all you need

The baby's first food is breast milk. If the mother's milk is not available, the baby can feed on formula, which is artificial milk similar to breast milk. The newborn feeds frequently, often every two to four hours. Smaller babies feed more frequently, as the tiny stomach cannot hold much milk. Babies do not overfeed on breast milk.

The baby's sucking produces a hormonal response in the mother's body, which triggers the production of more milk. Breast milk is rich in protein, sugars, and the vitamins and minerals the baby needs. It contains fats essential for the development of the brain, eyes, and **nervous system**. The baby's brain is still growing new neurons (brain cells) and is rapidly making connections between them. Without adequate nutrition, brain development does not take place properly. Breast milk also contains hormones, enzymes, and antibodies (proteins that kill agents of disease), which aid in development and protect against disease. These are not in formula.

"[Breast-feeding] has long-term effects in reducing the mean [average] level of blood pressure in adults. Adults who have been breast-fed have lower **cholesterol** *levels. It has benefits for the mother for reducing her risk for ovarian cancer and breast cancer."*

—Bernadette Daelmans, medical officer, Division for Newborn and Child Health and Development, World Health Organization

Tasty!

Sweet tastes generally appeal more to babies and children than to adults. Changing patterns of taste preference, from sweet to savory tastes, may help adults avoid weight gain from eating unnecessary sugars—although preferences vary among individuals. Babies respond to bitter tastes, but they do not register salty tastes for the first six months of life. The kidneys filter dangerous materials, waste, and water from the blood, but the immature kidneys cannot deal with salt. Feeding a baby salted food is dangerous, as it can lead to kidney damage and even death.

AMAZING BUT TRUE!

Tiny taste buds

The taste buds develop in the fetus at 20 weeks. A newborn baby has more taste buds than an adult, with some on the insides of the cheeks as well as on the tongue.

Taking control

Babies need to flex their limbs to help their muscles develop. They also need to experiment with making noises and to hear adults and children speak in order to prepare for speech themselves.

New babies have little control over their muscles. Babies gradually learn coordination by waving their arms and legs around and flexing their fingers and toes. In the first weeks of life, babies' neck muscles grow stronger, so that

Reflex actions

Some muscles respond by reflex. A reflex is an automatic action that the body takes in response to a stimulus. For example, a new baby held up with his or her feet just touching the ground will "step." This is a reflex action. Other reflexes help the infant survive—sucking is a reflex, as is searching for the nipple (called rooting). These ensure that the baby can feed immediately. After about two months, reflexive sucking ends and the baby will only suck if he or she wants to.

Starting to eat

The following is a timeline of how babies start to eat.

6–9 months	9–12 months	12–18 months	18 months–2 years
The body can start dealing with semi-solid food, soft foods such as mashed fruits and vegetables, and baby rice (finely ground rice) mixed with breast milk or formula.	The baby can eat a wider variety of food that is more coarsely mashed and try "finger foods" such as pieces of raw carrot and apple.	The baby is growing more teeth and can eat many foods that the rest of the family eats. There are still some foods the baby must not have, including nuts and extra salt.	The baby may become a fussy eater, unwilling to try new foods.

they can hold up, lift, and turn their head. The leg muscles need to develop before they can bear the body's weight for standing and walking.

The sphincter muscles that keep food in the stomach and waste in the bowel and bladder are weak at birth. Babies often vomit part of their food. They cannot control when they pass urine and excrement (solid waste). Conscious control of the bowel and bladder are usually learned in the second year.

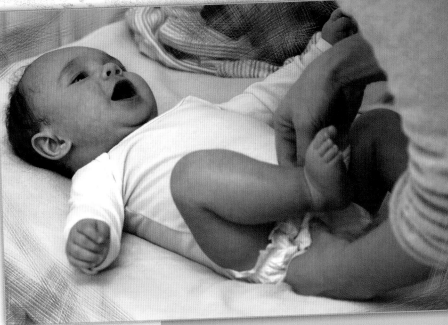

All clean
A baby can't control the bladder and bowel muscles and must wear a diaper. It's important to change this frequently to keep the baby clean.

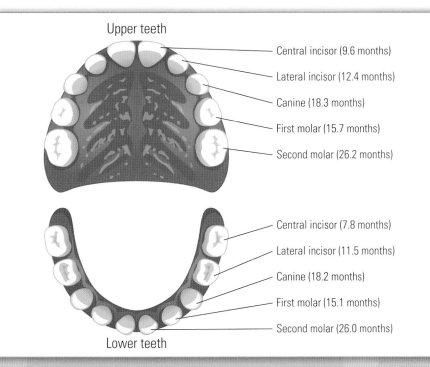

Upper teeth

Central incisor (9.6 months)

Lateral incisor (12.4 months)

Canine (18.3 months)

First molar (15.7 months)

Second molar (26.2 months)

Central incisor (7.8 months)

Lateral incisor (11.5 months)

Canine (18.2 months)

First molar (15.1 months)

Second molar (26.0 months)

Lower teeth

Growing teeth

A baby's first teeth start to emerge at 6 to 10 months. The baby starts to chew on things, which helps the process of new teeth cutting through the gums. This can be painful for the baby. The baby's teeth must be cleaned with a soft brush as soon as they emerge.

Teeth, in and out
This diagram shows the order in which teeth start to come through the gums, in the second half of the first year. They start to fall out, to be replaced by the permanent teeth, from around the age of six years.

How well can babies see?

People often say that babies cannot focus well and so cannot see properly. The baby's eyes can focus, but still the baby does not see well. Cells in the **retina** (the inside back surface of the eye), the nerves, and the area of the brain that deal with vision are not fully developed at birth. The young baby's vision is blurred. The nervous system matures over the first months of life, and by eight months old the baby's vision is almost as good as that of any adult with perfect vision. The final adjustments take place over the early years of childhood.

At around six to eight weeks, the baby's eyes will track a moving object. It is important for the baby to have lots of interesting things to look at and close contact with human faces, which encourages developing vision and engagement with the world.

AMAZING BUT TRUE!

Big baby eyes

Although newborn babies are only around 30 percent of their final adult height, their eyes are already 75 percent of their final size. That is why babies' eyes look so large.

Get up and go!

As babies develop stronger muscles and bones and better coordination, they become more mobile. By around six months, most babies can sit up for short periods. A little later, they learn to crawl or to shuffle on their bottoms. Soon after that, they start to pull themselves into a standing position and then begin to walk, at first holding on to things. Babies need a safe area to move in, with surfaces for pulling themselves up and holding on to as they move. All stairs must be blocked with a stair gate, and low windows must be barred and locked.

Spotting problems

Babies and children develop at different rates and reach milestones at different times. Even so, health professionals, parents, and caregivers need to watch each baby's progress. Developmental delays can be a sign that something is wrong. Spotting any problems early gives the best chance of treatment and putting in place the help the child will need. Tracking height and weight, testing hearing and vision, and looking out for milestones such as sitting, crawling, walking, and speaking help to reveal whether the baby is developing normally.

The knee bone's connected to...

The skeleton of a developing fetus is initially made of **cartilage** rather than bone. Cartilage is more flexible than bone. The skeleton hardens into bone as the fetus grows, but some bones—including the kneecaps—remain as cartilage until after birth. The kneecaps **ossify** (turn to bone) by the age of three years in girls and five years in boys. The newborn baby has around 300 bones, but some of these fuse together as the child grows (as do the bones in the skull). An adult has only 206 bones.

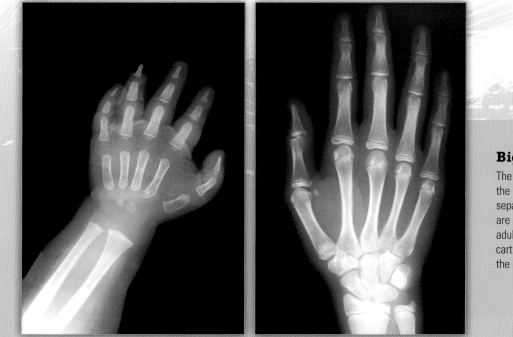

Bigger bones

The X-ray on the left shows the bones in a child's hand, separated by parts that are still cartilage. In the adult hand (on the right) the cartilage has ossified and the bones have joined up.

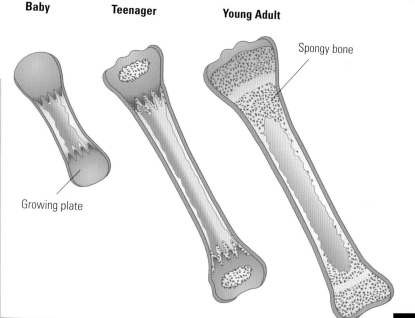

Baby **Teenager** **Young Adult**

Spongy bone

Growing plate

Hardening bones

The bones of the embryo have large areas called growing plates at each end. These contain cartilage (pink). As the child grows, more bone forms and the cartilage reduces. Cartilage is replaced by spongy bone tissue, which eventually hardens into solid bone. The adult bone has a small area of cartilage right at the end. (See page 24 for more on how bones grow.)

Case study: Being part of the world

A baby's physical needs must be met, but the baby also needs affection, stimulation, and engagement with other people. Babies who lack physical touch, love, and engagement with others do not make the necessary connections in the brain to form relationships and function normally later in life. It has been suggested that they become prone to depression, violence, addiction, self-harm, and other mental and emotional disorders.

AMAZING BUT TRUE!

Cuddles are good for you

In a hospital study of preterm babies, researchers found that babies who were handled on a regular basis grew almost 50 percent faster than others who were well cared for in all other respects, but experienced little human touch. Months later, the babies who were touched more were healthier.

"Scientific studies have shown that babies who are held and touched often during very young infancy, tend to have stronger immunity [defenses against disease], cry less often, gain weight faster, and develop more quickly."

—Karen Sullivan,
child care expert

Romanian orphanage babies

During the 1980s, unwanted children in the repressive state of Romania, in eastern Europe, were housed in cold, harsh orphanages. The children spent most of their time in cots, often without blankets. They were not held, cuddled, or talked to, even when feeding. Often they were washed under a cold faucet or left in filthy conditions for long periods of time. When the orphanages were opened to the world in 1989, the plight of the children attracted international attention.

Psychologists (people who study the human mind) and other medical workers studied the children and tracked their development after they were adopted or given more suitable care. Studies found that the severely neglected children had abnormally high levels of the hormone cortisol in their bodies. The body produces cortisol in response to stress.

Hungry for love

These children in a Romanian orphanage are starved of love and affection. A poor environment in the first year of life permanently affects brain development and the ability to speak.

That was not the only effect. Some children who had stayed in orphanages until they were 15 or even 20 years old had the physical appearance of children five or six years old. Although their food intake had been enough for them to grow normally, the lack of stimulation meant the children's bodies did not produce growth hormones. (See page 22 for more on this topic.)

Children in the orphanages suffered developmental delays in all areas. They often could not walk or talk at two or three years of age and did not know how to respond when touched or picked up by adults. When some children were taken out of the orphanages and placed with foster families, they began to recover. The younger they were when removed from the orphanages, the more quickly and fully they recovered, while those who stayed in the orphanages did not make similar progress. Even though the fostered children grew taller and heavier and learned to walk, talk, and interact, their heads remained unnaturally small and their brain activity stayed below normal.

Scientists concluded that head (and brain) growth can be severely and permanently affected by the wrong environment in the first year of life, and that the ability to speak is affected by conditions in the first two years of life.

The Growing Child

After the first few months of life, a baby becomes more active and begins to walk and talk, growing into a toddler and then a child. It is a time of rapid development in all areas.

The growing body

Growth happens in four stages. The first is before birth. In the second stage, babies grow very quickly in the first year, slowing down a bit in the second year. In the third stage, children grow at a steady rate of about 2 inches (5 centimeters) a year until just before puberty, when there is a final growth spurt. This fourth stage lasts until the end of puberty.

Babies usually gain half their birth height in the first year—so a baby born at 20 inches (50 centimeters) will be 30 inches (75 centimeters), or 2.5 feet, at 12 months. A girl is half her adult height at around 19 months, and a boy is half his adult height at 24 months. Babies double their birth weight in the first five months, triple it in the first year, and are four times their birth weight at the end of the second year. Weight gain slows down after that.

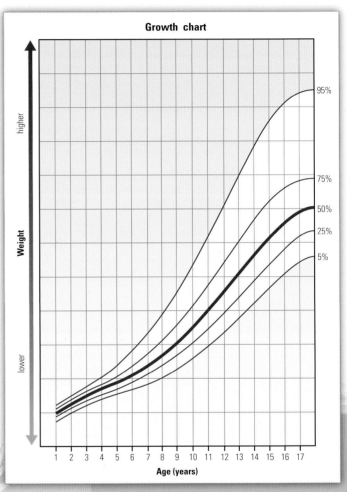

Growth chart

Keeping track

Medical professionals check the physical development of young children against charts that show the growth patterns of normal development divided into percentiles, which are percentages of children of a particular weight or height at each age. If a child does not follow the normal pattern of growth, there may be problems that need to be investigated.

Growing pattern

Percentile growth charts show bands in which children fall. The outer lines show the borders of normal size and development. Only 5 percent of children fall below the bottom line of this chart, and only 5 percent are above the top line.

The proportions of the body change as the baby grows up. At birth, the head accounts for about a quarter of the total length of the body, but an adult's head is only one-eighth of his or her height. A baby also has a large body compared to the length of the arms and legs. As the child grows, the arms and legs become longer more quickly than the torso, and so the child takes on more adult proportions.

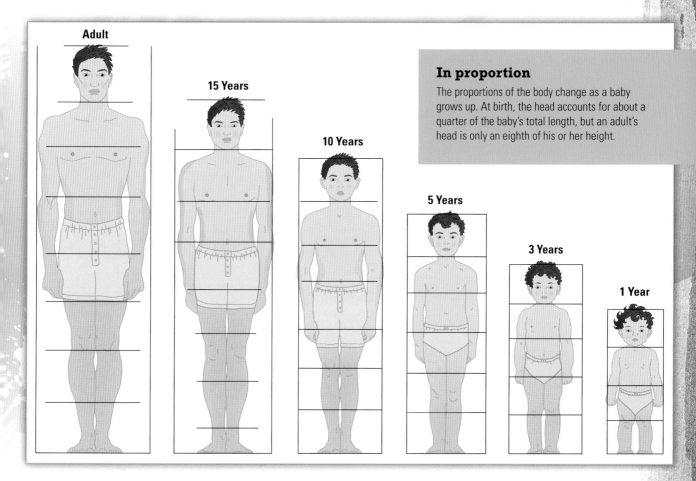

Adult
15 Years
10 Years
5 Years
3 Years
1 Year

In proportion
The proportions of the body change as a baby grows up. At birth, the head accounts for about a quarter of the baby's total length, but an adult's head is only an eighth of his or her height.

Fat and body shape

Fat stores energy and is broken down if we are short of food. But it also keeps us warm by trapping in heat. It is protective, too—it acts like a blanket wrapped around bones and organs to keep them safe from bumps and accidents. Some vitamins are also stored and moved in fat. Everyone needs some body fat, but too much is unhealthy.

Babies and toddlers often look chubby as they build up supplies of fat under their skin. A baby begins life with 13 percent body fat, but this rises to 20 to 25 percent in the first year. Older children of a healthy weight look slimmer. They have a thinner layer of fat beneath their skin. Once a child is using energy by moving around, there is less spare energy from food to store as fat and less need for insulation (keeping heat in), since movement helps the body to keep warm. Body fat levels drop back to around 13 percent by puberty.

How the body grows

Just as cells divide to make a fetus from a fertilized egg, they also divide in the growing body to make more cells. A dividing cell first makes copies of the chromosomes it contains. The two sets of chromosomes move to opposite ends of the cell. The cell then divides in two, making two cells with identical sets of chromosomes. As a child grows, the bones grow longer by reproducing bone cells, the skin grows larger by reproducing skin cells, and so on.

Growth takes a lot of energy and nutrients, so it is important that a growing child has a healthy diet. When children are short of food, they stop growing, as their bodies conserve energy for survival.

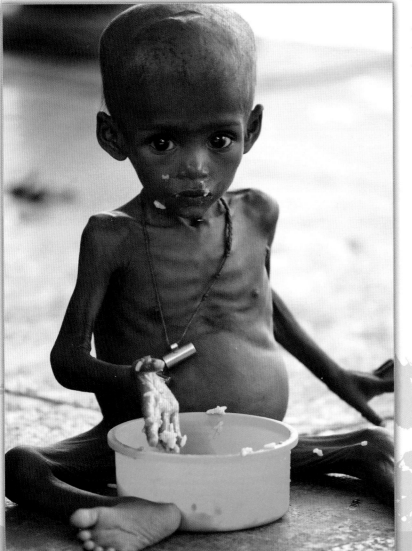

Food for growth

This child is suffering from malnutrition. His body will have stopped growing as all the energy he can gain from food is needed for survival. Now that he is in a relief camp with adequate food, he should start to grow.

Growth hormone

A child's growth is controlled by growth hormone. This is made in the **pituitary gland** just below the brain, and it travels around the body in the blood, triggering growth. It is produced throughout life, but it is most active in childhood. The pituitary gland also produces hormones that control the production of other hormones elsewhere in the body.

If children do not produce enough growth hormone, they may not reach a normal adult size. People with stunted growth and an adult height of 4 feet, 8 inches (147 centimeters) or less have dwarfism. Nearly three-quarters of people with dwarfism have a bone-growth disorder called achondroplasia, which causes short limbs. A body that has normal proportions but is smaller than average overall is caused by growth hormone deficiency (GHD).

A child with GHD is usually offered daily injections throughout childhood. After a few months, the injections produce growth and often increased strength, reduced body fat, and sometimes improved motor skills (control of movements like running and throwing). This helps the child to achieve a body that is normal for his or her age.

Case study: Getting growing

Sarina was born in November 2001, and was an average size—right in the 50th percentile. But she started to drop down the growth chart quickly in terms of physical development, even though her mental development was normal.

When she was 15 months old, Sarina's growth was not improving, and she was now off the bottom of the percentile growth charts. All medical tests came back normal. Her parents were desperate for a diagnosis so that treatment could start.

At four years old, Sarina was tested for GHD. Surprisingly, her levels were unusually high. One doctor noticed that high levels of GH combined with slow growth are signs of Laron dwarfism. This is caused by a lack of a different growth hormone, called IGF-1 (insulin-like growth hormone). Treatments for IGF-1 deficiency were very new, and Sarina's parents worried that there may be some risks. "No one ever died of being short," her father said, "but their quality of life suffers. We wanted a good quality of life for our daughter, so we went ahead with the treatment."

From 2007, Sarina has been having two injections every day. Her parents monitor the levels of sugar in her blood throughout each day, as diabetes is a risk for IGF-1 patients. Sarina is now growing well, and the outlook is good—she will probably achieve a normal adult height.

You cannot see inside

Children are not just smaller versions of adults. Some of their organs are not fully developed and cannot operate in the same way they do in an adult.

The liver has many roles, including removing poisons from the blood. The child's immature liver cannot deal well with some substances that are safe in moderation for adults. For this reason, children should only be given medicines recommended for a child of that age. Children can take small doses of acetaminophen or ibuprofen for pain relief, but they should not be given aspirin, which can lead to a dangerous condition called Reye's syndrome. The young liver cannot deal with alcohol, so children should not drink any alcohol at all.

Growing bones

By the time a child is two years old, the bones have ossified. Even so, they are still not as brittle as adult bones. If a child breaks a bone, it is often a "greenstick" fracture. The bone splits and breaks partially, in the same way a growing stick does not break cleanly.

The long bones inside the limbs grow from two areas near the ends of the bones called growing plates (see page 17). The new cells are cartilage cells. They push the existing cells toward the middle of the bone, compressing them and eventually replacing them with bone cells. When the bones have finished growing, around the end of puberty, the growing plates are converted to bone and stop producing new cells. After puberty, bone grows only if there is a fracture. First, cartilage forms, and then this is replaced by spongy bone tissue, which eventually hardens into solid bone.

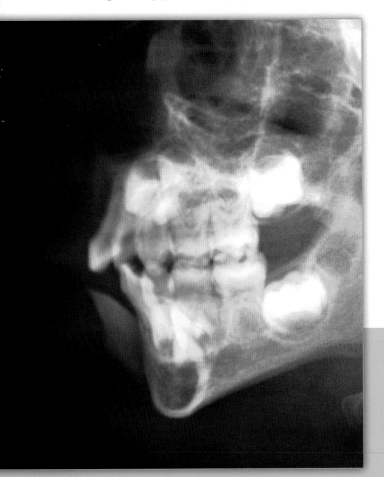

Teeth in waiting

In this X-ray of a child's jaw, the secondary (permanent) teeth are visible behind the primary teeth. Between the ages of 6 and 12, the permanent teeth push against the primary teeth, forcing them to drop out so that the new teeth can emerge.

Skin

Skin forms a protective layer between the body and the outside world. A child's skin is softer, thinner, and more fragile than that of an adult, but it is also more elastic and better able to heal itself. As an adult ages, the skin loses its elasticity and becomes thinner again.

Children's skin is easily damaged by the ultraviolet rays in sunlight. Damage appears first as burning on the surface of the skin, but after this has healed, other invisible damage to cells below the surface remains. Repeated sunburns in the early years greatly increase the risk of skin cancer and premature aging in later life.

AMAZING BUT TRUE!

Pointy or round?

Some cultures have molded children's heads by strapping them while the bones are still soft to make them flat, elongated, pointed, or more round. This practice shapes the head to make it more attractive, in the view of these people. Binding starts at about one month of age and continues for six months, while the bones of the skull harden. It is still done on the Pacific island of Vanuatu.

Skin deep

Skin is more complicated than it looks. The layer below the surface, the dermis, is filled with nerve endings, tiny blood vessels, sweat glands, and the roots of hairs.

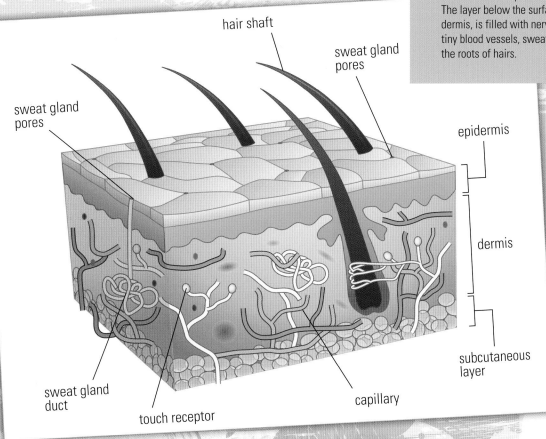

hair shaft

sweat gland pores

sweat gland pores

epidermis

dermis

subcutaneous layer

sweat gland duct

touch receptor

capillary

Teenage Changes

During **adolescence**, a child's body changes to a mature, adult body. It is a time of rapid change in many ways, all brought about and regulated by hormones.

Hormones act as chemical messengers that initiate changes in cells. They are produced in the body by groups of cells that form in **endocrine glands** (see diagram). Then they are released into the bloodstream, which carries them around the body. When they reach the cells they should affect, the hormones trigger a response. They have no effect on other cells.

Important endocrine glands

This diagram shows some of the important glands in the brain, kidneys, throat, and other organs. These glands release hormones into the bloodstream. For example, growth hormone is released by the pituitary gland and causes the liver to secrete further growth hormones.

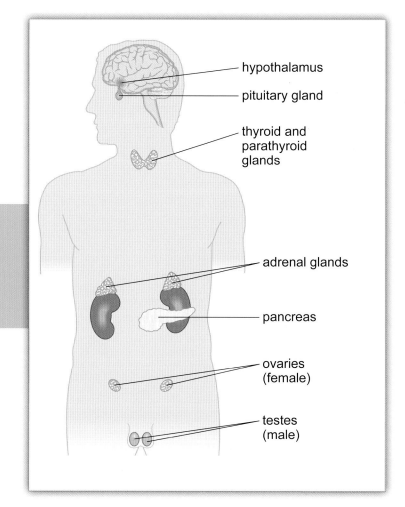

- hypothalamus
- pituitary gland
- thyroid and parathyroid glands
- adrenal glands
- pancreas
- ovaries (female)
- testes (male)

Hormones control activities such as growth, digestion, and reproduction, and they often have an effect on mood. Some of the more important endocrine glands in the body are the pituitary, pineal, thymus, thyroid, and adrenal glands, the pancreas, and the **ovaries** and **testes**.

The growth hormone that regulates the development of a child is released by the pituitary gland in the brain, and it causes the liver to secrete further growth hormones. As we have seen (see page 23), growth hormones are the most important hormones in the development of a child before puberty.

Girls and puberty

The following changes happen to girls during puberty.

Breast buds start to develop.

Puberty and hormones

Puberty is the point at which a child matures into an adult capable of reproduction. It can begin at any time from around 9 to 16 years of age, and it usually starts earlier for girls than for boys. Puberty starts when an area of the brain called the **hypothalamus** produces gonadotropin-releasing hormone. This travels to the pituitary gland (also in the brain) and stimulates it to produce two more hormones: **follicle**-stimulating hormone and luteinizing hormone. These travel in the blood to the ovaries in a girl or to the testes in a boy.

In a girl, the hormones trigger the release of **estrogen** and **progesterone** from the ovaries. Estrogen starts the process of puberty. Progesterone is released each month after **ovulation** and prepares the girl's body for pregnancy. In a boy, the hormones trigger the testes to release **testosterone**, which travels through the body and causes the changes that happen in puberty.

Both estrogen and testosterone stimulate the development of secondary sexual characteristics, such as facial hair in boys and increased body fat in girls.

What starts puberty?

Scientists do not know what causes the hypothalamus to set puberty in motion. It is affected by external factors, though, and body weight plays a part.

Puberty starts at different ages in different times and places. In the United States, the number of Caucasian girls starting puberty (with breast development) at age seven increased from 5 percent in 1991 to 10 percent in 2006.

Pubic and underarm hair starts to grow.

Breasts grow larger and the nipples grow larger.

The internal structure of the breast develops, with fat deposits and milk ducts growing.

Menstruation (monthly periods) begins (see page 28).

Menstruation: Preparing for pregnancy

Every month, a girl's ovaries release an egg, which travels along the **fallopian tubes** toward the uterus. The lining of the uterus thickens, ready to receive the egg. If the egg is fertilized, it implants in the uterus wall and begins to develop. If it is not fertilized, the uterus lining separates, and this and the egg are released from the body in menstruation. With the onset of menstruation, the girl is physically ready to become pregnant.

Cultural and social differences around the world mean that sexual activity is acceptable at different ages in different places. However, all teenagers should learn about contraception (practices to prevent pregnancy) and sexual health before the age at which they expect to have sexual relationships.

Boys' voices

In the past, boys with good singing voices were sometimes castrated (their testes were removed) to prevent the voice from changing with the release of testosterone. These men were called *castratos* and were unable to have children. This portrait shows the famous Italian opera *castrato* Farinelli, who lived from 1705 to 1782.

Changing voices

Men have a deeper voice than women or young boys. This is another change that comes with puberty. The larynx (voice box) grows larger during puberty and becomes visible as a lump in the throat called the Adam's apple. The larynx is a tube-shaped piece of cartilage in the neck. Thin muscles stretched around the larynx, called the vocal cords, also grow thicker and stronger. While the larynx is changing, a boy's voice can be unpredictably variable, and even squeaky, but once the changes are complete, his voice is permanently deeper.

Both the same

Some changes at puberty are the same in boys and girls. The skin starts to produce more oils and to grow more and coarser hairs. The extra oils can lead to blocked pores, blackheads, and acne—problems that are more common during adolescence than later in life.

The bones in the face grow longer, changing the shape of the face from the round shape characteristic of a child to a more adult, oval shape. This change is more marked in boys than in girls, but it happens in both.

What's that smell?

Children produce sweat to help control body temperature, but at puberty the body starts to make a different type of sweat at times of anxiety, stress, extreme emotion, and sexual excitement. It is thick and fatty and is produced only in the armpits, groin, nipples, ears, and navel. As bacteria on the body attack the sweat, it starts to rot and smell, causing body odor. To stay fresh, teenagers need to wash more frequently and thoroughly than small children.

Moody teens?

The mix of hormones in the teenage body can lead to mood swings and more extreme emotional effects, including depression, suicidal thoughts, and distorted views of the body (see pages 30 and 31). Teenagers' body clocks change, so they tend to stay up late and sleep late, finding it difficult to get up in the morning. A sense of adventure and desire for excitement leads many teenagers to experiment and some to engage in risky behavior.

Boys and puberty

The following changes happen to boys during puberty.

Testes grow larger. → Pubic hair starts to grow. → The penis grows larger and the voice begins to change. → Underarm and facial hair start to grow.

A distorted view

As teenagers become sexually aware, they often become more conscious of their bodies and how attractive they are. Sometimes this becomes exaggerated and leads to a distorted view of the body called body dysmorphic disorder (BDD). It can lead to eating disorders, insecurity, obsessive behavior, and other problems.

Two common eating disorders are anorexia nervosa and bulimia. People with anorexia reduce their food intake until it is so low they lose weight. They can become dangerously ill and can even die. Young people with bulimia do not stop eating, but rather eat a lot and then purge by throwing up or using laxatives.

People with eating disorders sometimes exercise excessively in an attempt to lose weight. Exercising a lot while taking little nourishment can be very dangerous. The body breaks down protein to get energy, and breaking down the protein in heart muscle can lead to a heart attack.

Case study: Thinner and thinner

Nineteen-year-old Carmel is from Oakland, California. She suffered from anorexia nervosa for three years. She describes the physical effects on her body, saying:

> "I was uncomfortable in my own body. I hated myself. I thought I was fat and thought that everything would be fine if I was thinner … I started skipping meals and if I ate much one day, I wouldn't eat the next day. Food was my obsession and my enemy. At one point I took six laxatives a day to make sure the little food I did eat would come straight out. My weight plunged and I was pleased. But I was just a shell—I felt nothing, thoughts slipped from my mind; I was the living dead. I could count my ribs, my periods stopped, my hair fell out, my face became pale and swollen."

Carmel recovered from anorexia after being admitted to the hospital and accepting medical help.

Mind and body

Girls with eating disorders may stop having periods, as the body interprets the lack of nutrition as a sign of food scarcity and so avoids pregnancy by stopping ovulation. Their **fertility** in later life can be reduced, even if they recover from the eating disorder.

Many young people with eating disorders often feel that their lives are out of control, and eating becomes one of the few things they feel able to control. The eating disorder may start with a catastrophic event, or a bout of depression or lack of self-esteem. This is one example of mental health problems leading to serious physical effects on the body.

All in the mind—but the mind is physical, too

Researchers in California asked people with and without BDD to look at photographs of other people's faces while monitoring their brain activity. They found different activity in the left and right sides of the brains of people with BDD, but no structural differences in their brains.

"This is the first time where there's evidence that there is kind of a biological abnormality that may be contributing to the symptoms—the distorted body image—in body dysmorphic disorder."

—Dr. Jamie Feusner, professor of psychiatry, University of California

The mirror lies

A person with BDD genuinely believes they have a different body shape from what they really have. They might look in the mirror and see a fat person when their weight is actually average or even too low.

All Grown Up: The Adult Body

The word "grown-up" suggests that adults have stopped growing, but that is not really the case. Although adults have stopped growing taller, they grow in other ways. Many parts of the body (such as the skin and hair) renew themselves, and some continue to grow larger throughout life.

Renewable bodies

Cells die and are replaced throughout most of the body. How long they last depends on the environment in which they are working. The lining of the stomach is constantly exposed to the acid and enzymes that help to break down food—a very harsh environment. So, the stomach lining is replaced every three to five days.

White blood cells last from a few hours to a few days, and red blood cells die after about 120 days. **Bone marrow** produces replacement blood cells all the time in response to need. It produces more white blood cells to fight infection and **platelets** to form a clot and scab after an injury. Hormones tell the body when to produce more cells of a particular type.

When does it stop?

Different parts of the body stop growing at different points. Our heads are nearly adult size by about the age of 10, but we stop growing taller when the long bones of the legs stop growing—at around age 18 for girls and in the early twenties for boys. Sometimes the feet continue to grow into the twenties. Even older adults often say their feet are getting larger. This is largely due to the feet spreading as they carry body weight.

AMAZING BUT TRUE!

No grow area

One part of the body that does not keep growing is tooth enamel. It is never renewed, so damage to the enamel from tooth decay is never naturally repaired.

Growing in places

The body adapts to how it is used. People who repeat an activity consistently find that their body adjusts, and so athletes develop strong, muscular legs, for example. This development can be unequal. For example, tennis players have one upper arm that is thicker and stronger than the other, because the muscle of their favored arm is built up wielding the racket.

Unlimited growth

This Sikh man's religion forbids him to cut his hair or beard. The length of his beard is limited by the time the hair follicles on his face stay active. When a follicle rests, the hair falls out.

Some things never stop!

The hair on your head will keep growing for your whole life (unless you lose it through baldness). If you never cut your hair, it would grow very long, although it breaks more readily with age. The hair on other parts of the body does not grow as long.

Each hair grows from the bottom, coming from a hair follicle. Each follicle works for a period, but then it rests and the hair falls out. When the follicle starts working again, a new hair grows. Follicles on the head can keep going for years at a time, so a single hair can grow very long. On other parts of the body, the follicle rests every two or three months, so the hairs are short when they fall out.

The nails and skin never stop growing. They are constantly worn away and renewed.

Fit bodies

The body of a young adult is usually at the peak of fitness. It is equipped for reproduction and for hard work. This is the time at which people often feel most comfortable in their bodies and enjoy an active physical life. The fitness of the body can be affected by lifestyle. Obesity, drug or alcohol misuse, eating disorders, self-harm, and other problems can all reduce health in adulthood.

There is no single description of the perfectly fit and healthy body. There are differences between males and females and among individuals. Some people naturally carry more fat than others, for instance, or are taller or shorter. People with disabilities may be very fit and healthy in most ways, but have particular parts of their bodies that do not work well. Fitness and health are best measured against individual potential, rather than by comparison with others.

Generally, men are more muscular than women, and women have more body fat than men. Women have fat around the hips and thighs, which men do not. Scientists think that this is an energy supply that can be drawn on when the woman needs to produce breast milk. From the age of around eight, girls gain fat much more quickly than boys. They do not create more fat cells, but the fat cells are larger and can store more fat. During adolescence, girls also lay down more fat cells. A woman of a healthy weight has around twice the body fat of a man of a healthy weight. Men's bodies are around 61 percent water, while women's bodies, having more fat, are about 52 percent water.

Unrestrained

South African sprinter Oscar Pistorius is extremely fit and healthy even though he does not have lower legs. Fitness and health are not constrained by disability.

Nature and nurture

The adult body is the result of both genetic and environmental factors. We all have an individual genetic makeup that controls many aspects of our appearance and health. But inherited characteristics can be changed to some degree by how we live and by how our mothers lived before we were born. If you have inherited blue eyes, this will not be changed by what happens to you. But people with a tendency to be very tall will not achieve their full height if they are not given healthy food during childhood.

Some people have a genetic tendency to develop particular diseases. Whether they will develop them or not often depends on how they live. Adequate nutrition, exercise, sleep, and an emotionally stable life are important in staying healthy.

Case study: Avoiding breast cancer

Karen was 40 years old when she discovered that many of the women in her family had suffered from breast cancer and some of them had died of it. An aunt told her that she had been genetically screened and had a mutation (change in structure) on one of her genes that gave her an increased chance of breast cancer. Karen had the test, too, and was able to adjust her lifestyle to reduce the chances of the cancer developing. She has frequent checkups, so that if cancer does emerge, she will spot it at an early stage, when it is easy to treat.

AMAZING BUT TRUE!

Disabled?

Oscar Pistorius (pictured) was born with major bones missing in each of his legs, and had to have both legs amputated before he had learned to walk. As a young child, he learned to walk using prosthetic (artificial) legs. By his teen years, he was playing a wide variety of sports including tennis, rugby, and triathlons. In 2004, he began racing as a sprinter using the flexible prostheses seen in the photo. Since then he has broken sprinting world records and won four gold medals in the Paralympic Games. He made history competing against the world's best runners at the London 2012 Olympics, reaching the semi-finals.

The next generation

The body is best prepared for reproduction in early adulthood. A woman's fertility starts to reduce a little as she approaches 30, and it drops after 30 until it ends with **menopause** (see page 38). As a woman ages, her chances of getting pregnant reduce and the chance of having a child with health problems increases. A man's fertility starts to decline around age 40, but it drops more slowly—even a man in his seventies can father children.

Growing a new human

Pregnancy results when an egg released in the woman's body is fertilized by a sperm cell. The fertilized egg starts to divide before it implants in the uterus and produces a hormone, human chorionic gonadotropin (HCG), which prepares the lining of the uterus to receive the fertilized egg. When the fertilized egg touches the lining, some of the cells start to grow into it to make the placenta. During pregnancy, the placenta releases hormones that affect the mother's body.

Pregnant and healthy

Although sometimes the hormones produced by the placenta make a woman sick during pregnancy, the body is generally healthy and fit. Many women feel better than ever!

AMAZING BUT TRUE!

Fertility in men

A fertile man produces 1,000 new sperm every second. Any sperm that are not ejaculated (released from the body) after around 70 days are reabsorbed.

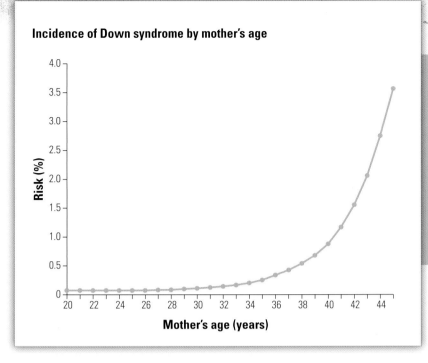

Incidence of Down syndrome by mother's age

Risking risks

The chance of having a baby with Down syndrome, a disability caused by defective genes, is low while a woman is young but increases rapidly as she approaches menopause. At age 45, the chance is greater than 3.5 in 100.

Fertility problems and treatments

One in 7 couples has fertility problems. Infertility has many causes. Hormonal treatments can encourage the woman to ovulate or make the womb more receptive. Artificial insemination involves putting sperm directly into the woman's reproductive system artificially, using donor sperm if her partner's sperm is faulty. If an egg is fertilized, the pregnancy follows the usual course. IVF (in vitro fertilization; see the box) involves taking eggs from the woman and combining them with the man's sperm outside the body, then putting fertilized eggs back into the woman's uterus to grow.

Case study: An IVF baby

Emily, 28, and Alfie, 29, tried unsuccessfully to conceive for two years before seeking medical help. Doctors found that both of Emily's fallopian tubes were blocked. Alfie's sperm count was normal, so his sperm could be used to fertilize Emily's eggs.

Emily was given injections of fertility drugs to prompt her ovaries to release eggs. She had to go for three ultrasound scans to check on the development of the eggs, and when they were ready, she went into the hospital for a day and had nine eggs removed. Five eggs were combined with Alfie's sperm, and two fertilized eggs grew successfully into early embryos. After three days, one was put back into Emily's body, and she had a successful pregnancy. Emily donated the eggs not needed for her own treatment to help women who do not produce eggs.

Midlife changes

Midlife is a time of further changes in the body. For a woman, menopause marks the end of the time when she can have children.

Menopause

A woman's body undergoes considerable changes in midlife, called menopause. This usually happens between the ages of 45 and 55. By the end of menopause, the woman no longer has periods, no longer releases monthly eggs, and cannot conceive children naturally.

Menopause occurs when the ovaries reduce their production of the female sex hormones estrogen and progesterone. There are often unpleasant side effects to these changes in hormone levels, including physical effects, such as hot flashes and sweating, as well as psychological and emotional effects, including anxiety, depression, and forgetfulness.

Hormone replacement therapy

Some women choose hormone replacement therapy (HRT) to reduce the unpleasant symptoms of menopause. HRT involves taking estrogen and progesterone supplements to replace the hormones that the body is not producing. HRT reduces symptoms such as depression and hot flashes, and it lowers the risk of some conditions common during and after menopause, such as thin, brittle bones (osteoporosis) and cancer of the colon and rectum. HRT does not prolong menstruation.

Menopause timeline

Menopause varies a lot between individual women, but many women follow this general pattern.

Perimenopause

(The phase before menopause in the early and mid-forties, to late forties and early fifties)

- Periods become less regular and some are missed.

- Hot "flashes"—periods of suddenly feeling very hot, lasting minutes or hours—occur, as do night sweats.

- Breasts are painful or sensitive.

Menopause

(Late forties and fifties)

- Periods become much less regular and then stop.

- Night sweats and hot flashes continue.

- Mood swings, difficulty thinking, and sleeplessness are issues.

- There are reduced secretions in the vagina, causing dryness and infections of the urinary tract.

Post menopause

(The fifties onward)

- Periods have stopped completely.

- There is a reduced desire for sex.

- Night sweats and hot flashes stop a few years after periods end.

Men also experience emotional and psychological changes in midlife, sometimes called male menopause. Some doctors think this may be the result of lowering testosterone levels, but there is no marked decline that is comparable to the hormonal changes in women's bodies. It is possible that the anxiety and associated behavior in men is the result of worry about aging and of reflecting on what they have achieved (or not achieved) in their lives so far.

Changing shapes

The body shape of both men and women changes in midlife. The waist thickens, and many people lay down extra fat, sometimes increasing their fat by up to 30 percent. Reduced activity contributes to weight gain—people take in as many calories in their food but use fewer in exercise, so the body lays down fat stores.

Muscles stiffen with age, making the body less supple. Some of the internal organs lose some of their cells, and muscles naturally atrophy (waste away) with age. Muscle changes begin as early as the twenties in men and the forties in women. Muscle cells do not replace themselves as readily, and may begin to shrink.

Midlife shapes

In middle age, people carry more fat but it's important to guard against gaining too much weight. Being overweight in midlife increases the risks of diabetes, heart disease, **stroke**, and cancer later. Obesity in middle age also makes people four times as likely to develop **dementia** in old age.

Hair and eyes

Many men and some women start to lose their hair in midlife. For example, in the United States, around two-thirds of men begin balding by the age of 60. This is caused by a hormone called DHT (dihydrotestosterone) produced in the hair follicles, testes, prostate, and adrenal glands. DHT causes the hair follicles on the head to deteriorate and eventually stop working. Baldness usually begins on the crown of the head or at the temples. This classic pattern of baldness is genetically determined and runs in families.

Even if it does not fall out, hair usually changes color in both men and women. Some hairs lose their pigment, growing white. In previously dark hair, this looks gray, as the colored and white hairs are mingled together. As more hairs fall out and new hairs grow without pigment, the hair becomes increasingly gray and eventually white.

Most people develop farsightedness (presbyopia) in midlife. The lens in the eye becomes stiffer and loses its power to focus light on to the retina. So, distant objects appear clear, but things nearby look blurry. Many middle-aged and older people need to wear glasses to read or do close work.

Black and white

This man's hair and beard are a mix of black and white—pigmented and unpigmented—hairs.

Healthy midlife

A healthy diet and continuing exercise are important for maintaining health in midlife. People in midlife are often less active than young people, but they do not always adjust their food intake. Some people give up sports and other exercise as demands on their time grow. Career success puts many people in less active jobs, and increasing wealth leads them to drive rather than walk or bike. Only 1 in 4 adults in the United States gets enough exercise to stay healthy, and 17 percent get no exercise at all.

Country	Percentage of adults who are overweight or obese	World ranking
Nauru, South Pacific	95%	1
United States	78%	9
New Zealand	68%	17
United Kingdom	61%	28
China	31%	148
Japan	27%	163
India	17%	176

Measuring obesity

Examine the chart above to see how selected countries compare in terms of body weight statistics. A BMI (body mass index) chart such as the one shown here is a tool that is often used to calculate body weight statistic. BMI is a measure of healthy weight. The calculation is weight (in pounds) divided by height (in inches) squared, and then that number is multiplied by 703. Obese people have a BMI of 30 or over; a BMI of 25 to 30 is considered overweight.

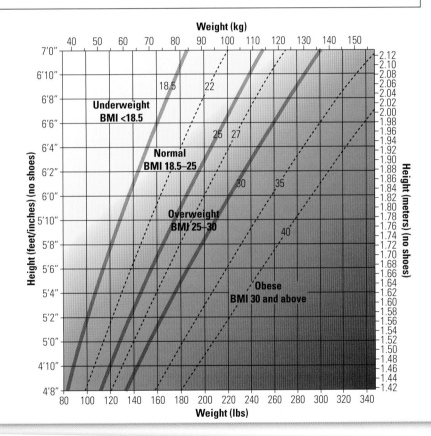

AMAZING BUT TRUE!

Malnourished and overweight

People can be malnourished if they eat too little food and also if they eat too much of the wrong kinds of food. Many people who are overweight or **obese** are also malnourished, because their diet contains too much fat and sugar but too few nutrients.

When Things Go Wrong

Few people make their way through life without illness or injury. Illness can be the result of infection, damage to the body, or something going wrong from within. Injuries might result from accidents or develop slowly over time.

Why does it hurt?

If you injure yourself, it usually hurts. Skin, bones, joints, muscles, and some internal organs have nerve endings that enable you to feel pain. When tissue is damaged, cells release chemicals that trigger an electrical impulse along the pain-detecting nerve. The impulse travels to the brain, where it is interpreted as pain. Painkillers work by blocking this message to the brain.

Pain is part of the body's protection mechanism—if something hurts, we learn to avoid it. But pain cannot always teach us useful lessons. For example, the pain of cancer does not help us avoid more pain.

Immediate response

The body responds as soon as an injury occurs. The blood contains red blood cells, white blood cells, and platelets. If the skin is cut enough to bleed, platelets move to the scene of the injury. They stick to a mesh of a protein called fibrin, which is also carried in the blood. The plug of fibrin and platelets becomes a clot and then a scab, which prevents bacteria from entering a cut. The bone marrow produces more platelets to replace those that have been used up and blood cells to replace those lost through bleeding.

AMAZING BUT TRUE!

Growing and regrowing

Did you know that the body's ability to heal reduces with age? A small child can regrow the tip of a finger that is cut off, but an adult cannot. Elderly people heal much more slowly than younger people. A fetus can regrow any part damaged in the womb. It does this using a combination of stem cells and something called the extracellular matrix, which helps the body lay down a framework on which tissue is built. This stops working soon after birth.

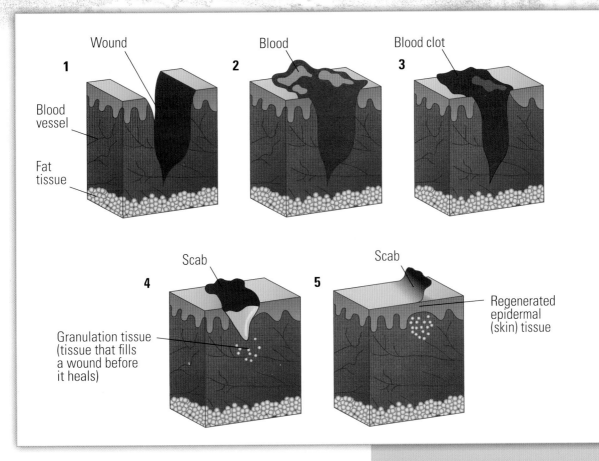

1 Wound · Blood vessel · Fat tissue

2 Blood

3 Blood clot

4 Scab · Granulation tissue (tissue that fills a wound before it heals)

5 Scab · Regenerated epidermal (skin) tissue

Healing

After an injury, the body cleans up the site of the wound before starting to rebuild the tissue. Dead cells, bacteria, and debris are destroyed by white blood cells and removed in the lymph, which is a clear fluid that collects from the tissues. The area around the injury looks red and feels hot as blood flow to it increases.

The growth hormone that prompts the young body to grow also instructs the body to repair injuries. Most tissue in the body consists of cells held on a framework of the protein **collagen**. If the collagen framework is intact, the cells can regenerate to fill the spaces left by damaged cells. If necessary, a new collagen framework is laid down and then new cells of the right types grow to fill the framework.

Finally, the collagen structure is remodeled as necessary. Any spare cells that are involved in repair but no longer needed self-destruct and are removed by white blood cells.

From cut to scab

When the skin is cut (1), blood wells up (2), but it soon starts to clot (3) and form a scab (4). This protects the body, stopping harmful dirt and bacteria entering the wound while the skin is repaired from beneath (5). The scab falls off when healing is complete.

Making it better

Medical intervention after an injury can help the healing process. Stitching or sticking the edges of wounds together helps to protect against infection, promote healing, and prevent large scars. A new development in medicine uses an artificial collagen template to encourage cells and blood vessels to grow in a damaged area.

Modern medicine can often provide prostheses—artificial replacements for parts of the body damaged by injury or disease. Prosthetic limbs are false limbs; hidden prostheses include artificial valves in the heart and replacement joints. Many people have hidden prostheses, such as artificial valves in the heart or replacement joints.

Scarring

Serious wounds produce scars. A scar appears when the collagen produced to repair an injury lays down fibers in a different pattern from the original collagen. Scar collagen is arranged in bundles lying in one direction held with crosslinks, whereas normal collagen has a more random weave. Scar tissue on the skin does not grow hair follicles or sweat glands. In some cultures, people have injured themselves on purpose to produce decorative scars as a form of body adornment.

Under the skin

A tattoo is created by adding ink under the dermis to change the color of the skin. This is a permanent change, though sometimes it can be reduced by laser treatment.

Case study: New for old

British soldier Corporal Andy Garthwaite, 24, lost his right arm in a grenade attack while he was serving in Afghanistan. In 2011, he was fitted with an arm that can respond to messages from his brain in just the same way that his original arm worked. He had to learn to control the pressure he exerted with his new hand, since he could easily crush items he picked up or hurt someone while shaking hands.

Doctors moved the ends of nerves that had once gone into his arm, moving them instead into the muscles of his back and chest. The brain sends electrical impulses to these nerves,

Degenerative injury

During a long life, the joints come under a lot of pressure, especially if a person is overweight. The ends of two bones that meet at a joint are cushioned by a pad of cartilage covering the ends of the bones, so that they can move smoothly. Osteoarthritis, or degenerative bone disease, happens when the pad of cartilage wears away. The bones then grind together, causing pain.

The most effective treatment for degenerative bone disease is replacing the joint with an artificial one. The ends of the bones are replaced with metal caps, and plastic replaces the cartilage.

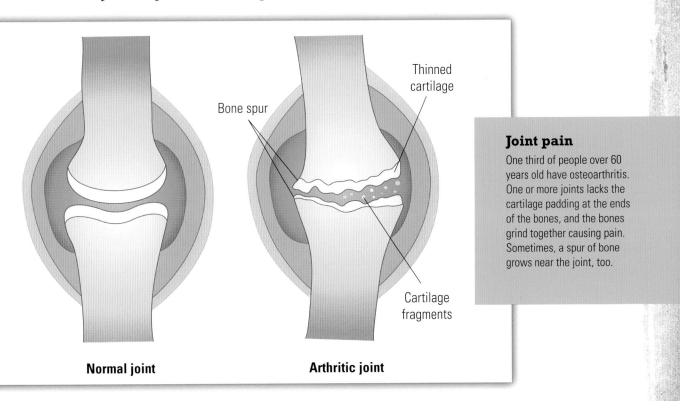

Bone spur

Thinned cartilage

Cartilage fragments

Normal joint

Arthritic joint

Joint pain

One third of people over 60 years old have osteoarthritis. One or more joints lacks the cartilage padding at the ends of the bones, and the bones grind together causing pain. Sometimes, a spur of bone grows near the joint, too.

and these impulses are picked up by the electrical circuitry of the prosthetic arm and instruct it to move.

Garthwaite says: "I think there are only five people in the whole world fitted with such a limb. It works by electronic pulses, and it will take between 16 and 18 months for me to learn how to control it … It's great—I mean I'm gutted [very sad] I lost my arm but I'm just thankful there's something out there."

The body turns on itself

Many illnesses are caused by microbes, which are tiny living things such as bacteria, viruses, or fungi. But some are caused by the body not working correctly. Cancer, diabetes, and **cardiovascular disease** (see the box) are the most common illnesses of this type.

Unhealthy hearts

Cardiovascular disease affects many older people. Arteries inside the heart, called coronary arteries, become "furred up" with deposits of fat. If there is so much fat that blood flow is reduced and not enough oxygen reaches the heart, it causes pain called angina. A lump of fat breaking off and blocking an artery causes a heart attack. If a blockage or blood clot blocks an artery to the brain, it causes a stroke. The brain is starved of oxygen, and brain damage results if the situation is not dealt with quickly.

Risk factors for cardiovascular disease include age, hereditary tendencies, smoking, obesity, a high-fat diet, high blood pressure, lack of exercise, diabetes, and a high level of cholesterol in the blood.

Cells usually reproduce as needed for normal growth, repair, and regeneration of tissues. When someone has cancer, cancerous cells continue reproducing unchecked. This can lead to lumps called tumors. Some types of cancer are caused by infection—for example, cervical cancer is caused by the human papillomavirus, and vaccination against this offers protection. Others are caused by environmental and lifestyle factors. For example, more than one-third of all cancer deaths in the United States are caused by smoking.

Treatments for cancer focus on killing the cancerous cells, either with chemicals (chemotherapy) or radiation (radiation therapy). Both these methods also kill normal cells, leading to very unpleasant side effects such as hair loss, exhaustion, and vomiting.

Checking for strokes

If someone suffers a stroke, immediate action is vital. FAST is a good way of remembering what to check for and what to do:

- **F**acial weakness: Can the person smile? Has their mouth or eye drooped?

- **A**rm weakness: Can they raise both arms?

- **S**peech problems: Can they speak clearly and understand what you are saying?

- **T**ime to call 911.

Smoking and cancer

Lung cancer is the most common lethal (deadly) cancer. Someone who smokes 25 cigarettes a day faces 25 times the risk of lung cancer as a nonsmoker. Even light smoking greatly increases the risk of dying of lung cancer. Smoking one to five cigarettes a day triples the risk of deadly lung cancer for men and increases it five times for women.

Diabetes and lifestyle

Diabetes occurs when the body either cannot produce the hormone insulin, which regulates the amount of sugar in the blood, or does not respond properly to the insulin. Diabetes can be a genetic condition or it can be caused by infection or damage, but it is increasingly brought on by lifestyle. Obese people have a greatly increased risk of developing diabetes. For example, just over one-quarter of people 65 years old and over in the United States have diabetes. Complications of diabetes lead to limb amputations (limbs being surgically cut off), kidney failure, heart disease, stroke, and blindness.

Illness and lifestyle

Many health problems, including cancer, diabetes, and cardiovascular disease, can be the result of an unhealthy lifestyle. Poor diet, smoking, drinking too much alcohol, misusing drugs, being overweight or obese, and lack of exercise can all contribute to health problems.

Some problems outside the individual's control can also lead to illness, such as emotional stress, poor living or working conditions, or exposure to pollution or toxins (poisonous substances).

Unhealthy lifestyles
Drinking alcohol, smoking, and sitting out in the sun without protection can all increase the risk of poor health in later life.

Case study: Asbestos

Asbestos is a material made of long mineral fibers. It does not burn, and it has been used in buildings as insulation (a substance that stops the movement of heat). If it is disturbed or broken up, asbestos produces dangerous dust. Breathing in asbestos dust can lead to respiratory diseases including asbestosis and a type of lung cancer called mesothelioma. There is long gap between exposure to asbestos and development of symptoms—anything

Graham's story

Graham worked as a heating engineer. As a young apprentice in the 1970s, he frequently had to strip old insulation material from buildings and pipes. Some of it contained asbestos, but the only protection he used was a paper mask. He was unaware of the dangers of breathing in asbestos dust. Graham left his job in 1981 and retrained as a mechanical engineer. Decades later, he visited his doctor because he was waking in the night feeling hot and sweaty and also losing weight. At first, he was diagnosed with stress and overwork.

When Graham developed breathing difficulties and chest pain in 2003, he went into the hospital with suspected pneumonia (lung inflammation). While he was there, X-rays and scans showed doctors that he might have asbestosis, and they asked Graham if he had worked with asbestos. Although he had not done so for 25 years, the asbestos had caused his problems. He was diagnosed with mesothelioma after doctors took biopsies (samples of tissue) from his chest. There is no reliable cure for mesothelioma, which is a form of cancer that attacks the lining of the lungs and chest cavity. It causes breathing difficulties, wheezing, chest pain, and persistent coughing, including sometimes coughing up blood.

For some time, Graham felt better, but with his diagnosis of mesothelioma he was not able to get work. In February 2006, he felt unwell and was admitted to the hospital again, but his health deteriorated quickly. One of the effects of the condition was anemia, a lack of red blood cells that leads to exhaustion. Graham could not take part in normal daily life with his family and felt increasingly sick. Treatments such as chemotherapy, radiation therapy, and surgery can sometimes help sufferers of mesothelioma, but they were not able to save Graham. He died six months later, leaving a widow and two teenage sons.

between 10 and 60 years. As the dangers of asbestos were not discovered until it had been in use for a long time, illness from past exposure is rising.

In the United States, 10,000 people die each year from diseases caused by asbestos. Asbestos is not banned in many countries, including the United States.

Help with breathing

A patient with advanced mesothelioma is often not able to breathe without technological assistance.

Winding Down

As people move into old age, their bodies change in many ways. Some people struggle with the changes of old age, but others enjoy their new freedom and the lack of stress.

Looking old

In many ways, older people look different from how they did when they were young. As the skin ages, it loses its elasticity and becomes wrinkled and thin. Age spots—areas of discoloration—often appear. Gravity causes some parts of the body to droop downward. Elderly people often have drooping ears, noses, breasts, and folds of skin. Their bodies look shorter, and a curving spine may make them stoop (see page 51).

There are two different aspects of aging. Intrinsic aging happens to everyone as time passes. Extrinsic aging is avoidable; it is caused by external events and lifestyle.

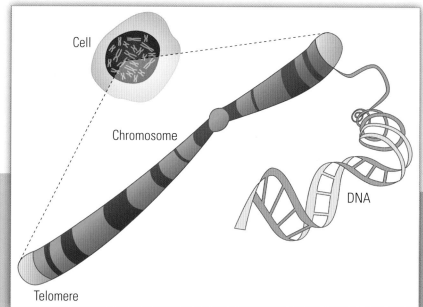

Cell

Chromosome

DNA

Telomere

Safety buffer

Every cell in the body contains chromosomes, and every chromosome ends with a telomere—a sort of safety buffer that protects the genetic information from loss as the chromosome shortens with copying.

The body's time bomb

Although we continue to grow new tissue throughout our lives, our cells can reproduce a limited number of times before the copies are faulty and do not function properly. Each chromosome has an extended end that contains no essential genetic information. This is called a telomere. Each time the cell is copied, part of the telomere is lost. Eventually, all the telomere has gone, and the genetic information at the end of the chromosome begins to be lost, leading to faulty cells.

Experiments with animals show that if telomeres are preserved, the animal lives much longer—from double to 10 times its normal lifespan. In cancer cells, the telomeres never shorten, so cancer cells live forever.

Aging skin

The skin is supported by a framework of collagen, but production of collagen slows down after middle age. A protein in skin called elastin, which makes skin springy, also decays with age. These changes make the skin become slack and wrinkled. In addition, the layer of fat beneath the skin is often lost in old age, giving the face a hollow or sunken look. These are intrinsic changes.

Changing looks

This woman shows several signs of aging, including white hair, loss of facial hair (eyebrows), and wrinkled skin.

The effects of sunlight on the skin cause extrinsic aging. Sunlight slows the production of collagen, breaks down existing collagen, and damages elastin, leading to premature wrinkles and saggy skin. It also discolors the skin, causing freckles and age spots.

Body structure

Elderly people often become shorter as the discs of collagen between the vertebrae (the small bones of the backbone) are compressed, reducing the length of the spine. Stooping, which can result from muscles in the back deteriorating, also makes a person shorter. The alignment of the hips and the knees changes, and this reduces the height further. As the body becomes shorter, the arms and legs look longer by comparison.

AMAZING BUT TRUE!

Return to youth

Ellen Langer of Harvard University carried out an experiment with a group of elderly men. She re-created the 1950s (the time period when the men had been young) with furniture, newspapers, music, and food. Over a week, signs of aging in the men seemed to reverse. The men looked younger, their joints became more flexible, their posture straightened, and their fingers became longer. There is not yet a scientific explanation as to why this happened, and more research is needed.

Slowing down

From some time in their forties, people are usually less active and need less food. So, if they eat as they did before, they become overweight. The muscles change with age, becoming stiffer, so sometimes endurance (the ability to be active for long periods) increases while flexibility decreases. For this reason, even quite elderly people can run marathons, but they are not supple enough to do gymnastics. Older people often get tired more easily.

Although the physical changes are distressing in some ways to older people, other changes are often welcome. Many older people, who may have retired from active employment, talk about feeling relief at no longer having to worry about being competitive in a work or social context or needing to attract potential partners. They also enjoy having free time and often take pleasure in grandchildren.

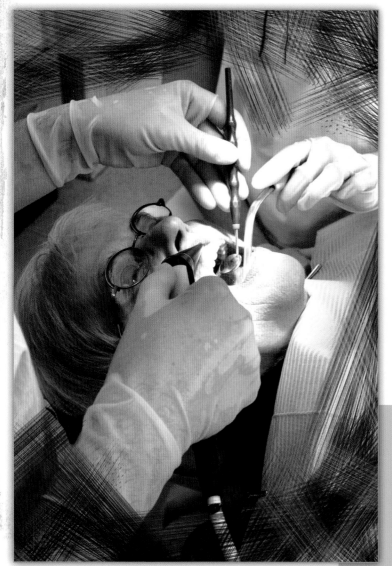

Declining senses

Many parts of the body work less well as people age. By the age of 60, many people have lost half their taste buds. Elderly people often complain that their sense of taste has deteriorated. It is important when caring for older people to make sure that they eat enough. If they do not feel hungry and do not enjoy food, they can quickly become malnourished.

Healthy old age

It is important for elderly people to continue having health checks, such as visiting the dentist and ophthalmologist (eye doctor) as teeth and eyes continue to change and need care in old age.

Most older people are farsighted, and some develop cataracts (clouding of the lens) or other vision problems. Teeth can become loose as the gums recede, and as the enamel thins teeth look yellower (revealing the yellow of the dentine beneath) and develop cavities more easily. Identifying eye disease and gum disease early through regular checkups means they can be treated before they do too much damage.

Hearing also deteriorates with age. People hear sounds over a reducing range of frequencies and often have difficulty hearing low-volume sounds or picking out speech in noisy surroundings.

How Alzheimer's disease works

Alzheimer's disease is caused by "plaques" or plates of a different protein forming on the outside of nerve cells in the brain, and by a protein that has been badly formed and deposits in tangles inside the nerve cells. Both of these cause nerve cells to die, leading to progressive loss of mental function.

Around a quarter of the world's population is thought to have a gene that can lead to the development of Alzheimer's. Symptoms usually start in middle age (before the age of 60).

Confusion and dementia

Many elderly people suffer from mental confusion, forgetfulness, or dementia. Some memory loss is common and normal in old age, but serious mental impairment is a feature of dementia and of conditions such as Alzheimer's disease (see the boxes). Elderly people with Alzheimer's or dementia sometimes become uncooperative and even violent and abusive. Medication can sometimes slow or manage dementia, but there is no cure.

AMAZING BUT TRUE!

Alzheimer's disease and dementia

The following are facts and figures about dementia:

- Sixty-two percent of people with dementia have Alzheimer's disease.
- There are 5.4 million people in the United States living with Alzheimer's. It is the sixth most common cause of death.

Taking care

Older people have more brittle bones than younger people, so they can easily break a bone if they fall.

They are also prone to getting cold, since they are less active and so generate less body heat than younger people. Some medications, including those for diabetes, can reduce the body's response to low temperatures. For these reasons, accommodation for elderly people should be heated to 68 degrees Fahrenheit (20 degrees Celsius). Wearing several layers of loose clothes, a hat, scarf, and mittens—even indoors—helps to keep the body warm.

The end of life

Eventually, everyone dies. The body cannot continue to repair itself and maintain the essential life processes. Sometimes death is sudden, but often a person's final days need special care.

End-of-life care is a special area of medical care. It begins when someone has a terminal illness or is frail and not expected to live long. It provides pain relief and treatments to alleviate distressing symptoms, as well as emotional and spiritual comfort.

Danger signs: Hypothermia

Hypothermia happens when the core body temperature falls below 95 degrees Fahrenheit (35 degrees Celsius). (Normal body temperature is 98.6 degrees Fahrenheit, or 37 degrees Celsius.) Anyone caring for an elderly person should recognize the signs of hypothermia, which are not always obvious. Below 93.2 degrees Fahrenheit (34 degrees Celsius), shivering slows and then stops, and at 84.2 degrees Fahrenheit (29 degrees Celsius), the body stops trying to generate extra heat or prevent heat loss. Sometimes people curl up, and they might hide because the brain has a burrowing instinct. They might even remove their clothes as they become confused.

A healthy old age

A nutritious diet, exercise, meaningful relationships with other people, and a sense of purpose in life help to keep elderly people healthy and happy, even if physical problems limit their activities.

Death happens when the body finally closes down. The heart stops beating and breathing stops. With modern medical care, someone whose heart and breathing have stopped can often be resuscitated (brought back to life), but this is not usually attempted if death is expected. When brain activity stops, the person is irreversibly dead. The brain cannot make a complete recovery if it remains without oxygen (carried in the blood) for more than three minutes.

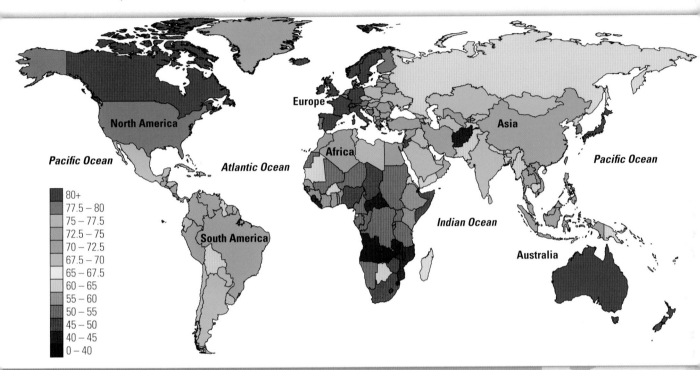

	80+
	77.5 – 80
	75 – 77.5
	72.5 – 75
	70 – 72.5
	67.5 – 70
	65 – 67.5
	60 – 65
	55 – 60
	50 – 55
	45 – 50
	40 – 45
	0 – 40

Worldwide life expectancies

This map shows how long, on average, people live in different parts of the world. There is a clear difference between economically developed areas such as North America, Europe, and Australia and less economically developed areas. The poorest countries, in parts of Africa, have the lowest life expectancies.

Life from death

Although each death is a sad event, it can also bring benefits to the living, particularly if the person dies young. Organ donor programs exist in many countries to give lifesaving surgery to people who need transplants. Body parts that can be used in transplant operations include the heart, lungs, kidneys, liver, cornea (from the eye), pancreas, intestine, stomach, hand, and face.

"We were also overwhelmed with gratitude for the person who agreed to organ donation and offered our child the gift of life ... It is such a wonderful thing to do for others ... After the transplant she got her life back. She was able to live life like a normal, healthy teenager."

—Bev, mother of a teenager who received a liver transplant in 2010

Quiz

Find out how much you remember about the growing and changing body by completing this quiz. You will find the answers on page 63.

True or false?:

1. If your teeth decay, your body can grow new enamel to fix the damage.

2. You keep growing connections between brain cells throughout your life.

3. A baby can be toilet trained at any age. It just takes longer to teach a small baby to do something.

4. A young baby has a better sense of taste than his or her grandparents.

5. If you never cut your hair, it would continue growing longer forever.

In your own words:

6. There are 206 bones in the adult body, but a baby has more than 300 bones. What happens to the extra bones?

7. If you have a serious injury, a surgeon might give you a skin graft, moving skin from another part of your body, to help the wound heal. Why is this better than letting your body grow scar tissue?

8. If a man has a low sperm count, how might he and his partner be able to have a baby?

9. Carla's grandma has given her a dress she used to wear as a young woman because "the dress is too long for me now." Why?

10. Omar is 75. He grumbles that his teeth have turned yellow. Why is this?

Choose an answer:

11. At what age is a person's head one-eighth of his or her height?

    a.) four years   b.) ten years   c.) adult

12. Which of these is NOT a problem associated with obesity in middle and old age?

    a.) diabetes   b.) cardiovascular disease

    c.) lung cancer   d.) osteoarthritis

13. Which part of the body keeps growing in adulthood?

    a.) teeth   b.) nails

    c.) bones   d.) intestines

14. At which age does a human have stem cells that are most useful to science?

    a.) before birth   b.) as a baby

    c.) just before puberty   d.) during puberty

15. Which of these might NOT cause growth problems in a child?

    a.) deficiency of a hormone   b.) lack of food

    c.) lack of affection and physical contact   d.) repeated sun damage

AMAZING BUT TRUE!

The oldest part of a body

Tooth enamel cannot renew itself. Indeed, the enamel on your adult teeth now will still be there when you are 80 or 90 years old. It began to grow when you were a fetus, and the enamel-making cells died when the teeth emerged.

Timeline: Growth Before Birth

The age of a fetus is counted from the date of conception, but the length of pregnancy is counted from the date of the woman's last period, so it is two weeks longer. If you look at books or web sites about pregnancy, you will need to remember the difference between the age of the fetus and the length of the pregnancy.

The following chart shows the different steps in the development of a baby.

10 weeks
1.7 inches (43 mm)

The fetus can swallow the amniotic fluid that surrounds it and produce urine. All the major stages of development are complete.

9 weeks
1.2 inches (30 mm)

The fetus can move, but the mother cannot yet feel its movements.

12 weeks
3.1 inches (80 mm)

The fetus is growing soft, downy hair called lanugo all over its body. The fetus can suck, yawn, stretch, and make different facial expressions.

16 weeks
4.7 inches (120 mm)

The chest moves up and down, practicing for breathing. The teeth start to form. Sweat glands develop.

38 weeks
20 inches (51 centimeters)

The lungs are fully developed, and all the instincts needed for survival (such as sucking and breathing) are in place. The baby is ready to be born.

25 days

The partly developed heart begins to beat.

30 days

0.2 inch (5 mm)
(measured from head to rump)

The beginnings of all organs and limbs have formed, and there is an early form of eyes and ears and the beginnings of the mouth.

7 weeks

0.9 inch (23 mm)

Eyelids are forming and will remain closed until 24 weeks. All the main organs and body structures are in place, although they are not fully developed.

5 weeks

0.4 inch (10 mm)

Fingers and toes have grown, and the fingers have fingerprints. The ears and eyes have developed. The fetus weighs about 0.04 ounces (1 gram).

18 weeks

10.2 inches (26 centimeters)
(now measured from head to heel)

The fetus can hear sounds from outside the mother's body and is swallowing and digesting the amniotic fluid.

20 weeks

11 inches (28 centimeters)

Tooth buds are forming in the gums.

30 weeks

16.5 inches (42 centimeters)

The skin is wrinkled, but a layer of fat is forming beneath it. The baby will gain around half his or her birth weight in the last eight weeks.

26 weeks

15 inches (38 centimeters)

The baby will turn toward a bright light and can blink. The bones are nearly complete but are still flexible.

Glossary

adolescence period when a child's body matures and becomes an adult body

artery blood vessel that carries blood from the heart

bacteria very small living things. Some bacteria cause diseases, but most are harmless and many are helpful to the human body.

bone marrow soft tissue inside the bones. In the larger bones, it produces new blood cells.

cardiovascular disease disease that affects the heart and/or blood vessels

cartilage tough but flexible connective tissue; it provides the hard parts of the nose and ears

cell basic unit, or building block, of life. All living things are made of cells, and the smallest living thing has a single cell.

cholesterol type of fat that is necessary to the body but dangerous to health in large quantities

chromosome strand of DNA that carries a collection of genes and forms one of the "chunks" of genetic material

collagen protein that is the main component of connective tissue such as skin and muscle

dementia loss of mental abilities, beyond normal deterioration in memory as part of aging

diabetes condition in which blood sugar levels vary dangerously, caused by the body not producing insulin or not responding properly to insulin

embryo developing, unborn baby from the point of conception until the end of the eighth week of development

endocrine gland part of the body that produces a hormone

enzyme protein that encourages a chemical reaction to happen in the body

estrogen female sex hormone

excretion process of removing waste from the body

fallopian tubes tubes which connect the ovaries to the uterus in a woman

fat complex chemical that is used in the body to store energy. Body fat is also a good insulator, keeping the body warm and cushioning organs and bones.

fertility ability to reproduce

fertilize bring together two sex cells (egg and sperm) so that the resulting cell can begin to grow into a new organism

fetus unborn baby after eight weeks of development (ten weeks of pregnancy)

follicle in hair, a group of cells forming a pit from which a hair grows

gene unit of heredity; it carries genetic instructions about a feature of a living thing, such as a person

genetic relating to the genes and heredity

hormone chemical used as a "messenger" by the body. The presence of a hormone triggers a response or action in a particular part of the body.

hypothalamus area of the brain that controls many functions of the body

joint place where two or more bones meet and the body can flex—as at the knee or elbow

menopause time in a woman's life when hormonal changes bring to an end the years in which she is able to reproduce

menstruation process of having monthly periods during which the lining of the uterus is shed

nervous system system of nerves and the brain

neural relating to the nerves

nutrient chemical obtained from food which is beneficial to the body

nutrition taking benefit from food

obese carrying a dangerously large amount of body fat, with a BMI of 30 or over

obesity state of being very overweight

ossify turn to bone

ovary part of a woman's body that produces eggs

ovulation release of an egg that is ready to be fertilized

pituitary gland small endocrine gland in the brain which releases many hormones, including those controlling growth and sexual development

placenta organ that grows from part of a fertilized egg into the woman's uterus to sustain the unborn baby as it grows

platelet type of blood cell that forms clots and scabs

preterm born before fully developed

progesterone female sex hormone

protein complex chemical that forms living things

puberty time during which the body becomes sexually mature

reproduction producing offspring; cells reproduce to create new cells, humans reproduce to create children

respiration chemical process of releasing energy from food. The term "respiration" is also used to mean breathing and gas exchange.

retina inside back surface of the eye, which has light-sensitive cells

sperm male sex cell that needs to combine with an egg to produce an embryo

stem cell cell that has not yet become a particular type of tissue

stroke medical condition in which blood supply to the brain is interrupted, often because of a blood clot blocking an artery

testes part of the male body where sperm are produced and stored

testosterone male sex hormone

tissue group of similar cells that makes up the structure of the body. There are different types of tissue, including skin, blood, bone, muscle, and nerves.

umbilical cord cord that connects the growing baby to the placenta in the uterus. It carries nutrients to the baby, in the mother's blood.

uterus womb; the space in a woman's body where a baby grows

Find Out More

Books

Ballard, Carol. *Keeping Fit: Body Systems (Do It Yourself)*. Chicago: Heinemann Library, 2008.

Jukes, Mavis. *The Guy Book: An Owner's Manual: Maintenance, Safety, and Operating Instructions for Boys*. New York: Crown, 2002.

Madaras, Lynda, and Area Madaras. *The "What's Happening to My Body?" Book for Boys*. New York: Newmarket, 2007.

Madaras, Lynda, and Area Madaras. *The "What's Happening to My Body?" Book for Girls*. New York: Newmarket, 2008.

Townsend, John. *101 Things You Didn't Know About Your Body (101)*. Chicago: Raintree, 2012.

Web sites

www.cdc.gov/ncbddd/childdevelopment
Learn more about child development from the U.S. Centers for Disease Control and Prevention (CDC).

www.girlshealth.gov/body
Find out how the female body changes during puberty, and how to stay healthy and happy.

kidshealth.org/kid/stay_healthy/index.html
KidsHealth offers a clear, fun guide to staying healthy, with illustrations and animations.

pbskids.org/itsmylife/body/index.html
This PBS site has information on a range of subjects, including eating disorders, alcohol, and puberty.

Places to visit

The Exploratorium
3601 Lyon Street
San Francisco, California 94123
www.exploratorium.edu
Learn all about the human body at this
museum.

The Health Museum
1515 Hermann Drive
Houston, Texas 77004
www.mhms.org
This museum offers interactive exhibits about
the body and health.

Topics to research

Exercising through the ages
How does exercising and keeping fit affect the body at different ages? What types of precautions
should people of different ages take when exercising?

Fighting disease
How does the body fight disease? Is there a difference in the way an infant, child, or adult body
responds to disease?

Nutrition requirements
How do the nutrition requirements of the body change as it develops from a baby to child, then to
an adult, and then into old age?

Quiz answers (see pages 56–57)

1) False. Tooth enamel starts to form in the fetus and never regrows.

2) True. Connections are made when you learn things—and you can continue learning things throughout life.

3) False. A baby is physically incapable of controlling the muscles needed to choose when to empty the bladder and bowel.

4) True. People lose taste buds as they get older.

5) False. When a hair follicle rests, the hair falls out. A new one starts to grow after a while.

6) Many of the bones fuse together as the child grows.

7) Scar tissue does not look the same as normal skin. It does not have hair follicles (so it does not grow hair) and does not have sweat glands.

8) They might have a baby using sperm from a donor.

9) Older people shrink as the spine compresses and curves.

10) Tooth enamel thins with age so that the yellow of the dentine beneath becomes more visible.

11) c.

12) c.

13) b.

14) a.

15) d.

Index